Pine Furniture
Our American Heritage

Kathryn M. McNerney

COLLECTOR BOOKS
A Division of Schroeder Publishing Co., Inc.

The current values in this book should be used only as a guide. They are not intended to set prices, which vary from one section of the country to another. Auction prices as well as dealer prices vary greatly and are affected by condition as well as demand. Neither the Author nor the Publisher assumes responsibility for any losses that might be incurred as a result of consulting this guide.

Additional copies of this book may be ordered from:

Collector Books
P.O. Box 3009
Paducah, KY 42001

@$14.95 Add $2.00 for postage and handling.

Copyright: Kathryn M. McNerney, 1989

This book or any part thereof may not be reproduced without the written consent of the Author and Publisher.

For Steven and Joan Fellows ....

who share my interest in heritage

Appreciation

After mailing a manuscript to the publisher, I have time to pause and reflect back on its preparation – of how and where I was able to find the materials I was seeking – the frustrations and discovery thrills of research – belatedly amused at the ups and downs of travel – the trepidation (at least to me sometimes) of approaching the Unknown for permission to photograph and question – and then to experience, without exceptions, a warmth of understanding and cooperation. There are others than those named herein (probably a few even unaware of it) who didn't realize the extent to which they helped me with casual conversations and often the sharing of their special treasures. To everyone ... Thank you.

Florida
Deltona
   Montgomery Appraisals and Antiques
Fernandina Beach
   Rosanna R. Oliver Antiques
Jacksonville
   Lamp Post Antiques, Inc.
Mandarin
   Bayard Country Store
Middleburg
   Robert Simon (for film developing)
Orange Park
   Brian and Shelley Tebo
   Claude and Rosie Bass
   Helen Berline
   Orange Park Antique Market
Pensacola
   Finders Keepers
   Florida Sunshine Shows
   Gran's Attic
   Martha's Market
   Veazie's Antiques

Georia
Cave Spring
   Country Roads Antique Mall
Coosa
   Thomas Antiques
Rome
   Kay Mathis
   Skelton's Red Barn Antiques

Louisiana
Franklinton
   Joan's Antiques
Lafayette
   The Brown House

Mississippi
Hattiesburg
   Vayda's Antiques

New York
Clarence
   Feltz Antiques
Hilton
   Ed Boeyink
Lewiston
   Lexington Square
   Mimi Pyne's Antiques
North Tonawanda
   Hearts and Hands
Ransomville
   Wayne and Audrey Orr
Wilson
   Country Barn Shop
   Whitney and Lois Barnum
Youngstown
   Sharon for listening and phoning

Tennessee
Murfreesboro
   Antiques Unlimited
   Gene and Marie Norris
   Marie's Antiques
   Mary and Don Shaw
   Mary's Antiques
   Murfreesboro Antique Mall

Virginia
Chesapeake
   Cobb's Gifts and Antiques

Values

IMPORTANTLY, values given are prices shown on sales tags of individual pine items in shops, flea markets, malls and at shows, as well as set by owners/collectors.

It probably never occurred to a harried frontiersman trying to build a few vital furniture objects in the little time left from his continually providing food and security to add his touchmark (sign) to the wood. Thus, with signatures rare on hand-fashioneds and later factory products just occasionally stamped, it is very difficult to date early pine, especially when for so many years in the counties there were few or no styles/patterns changes, while in the cities, pieces were undergoing constant variations. But one can research, checking for similars and look-alikes, attentive to regional characteristics as the distinctive Pennsylvania Dutch artifacts and that Shakers used iron for hinges and wood for joinings.

Names were supplied by owners. Generally, a cabinet is a cupboard is a chest ... all stemming from a basic cased (framed) idea. A cabinet may be so-called because it has all or partial glass doors, a cupboard because of its solid wooden ones. Later 1800's sideboards are called dining cabinets or even chests if an Empire influence dictates a solid front of drawers clear to the floor.

Prices may momentarily pause, then only advance, and a show booth of good old "country-flavored" pine furniture is indeed a heritage-viewing pleasure.

Contents

A Furniture Legacy From The Pines

Early colonists arriving at America's eastern seacoasts had long been keenly aware of the constant depletion of forests in their European homelands. They must have stared with profound gratitude at unrestricted miles of magnificent trees stretching to the horizons (as encountered by later settlers pushing on westward). Seemingly endless woodlots were everywhere, ready to be cut for burning, for tools and utensils, for homes, animals' shelters, mills, smithys, churches, trading posts, for vehicles, and bridges for land and water transportation. Importantly, earnestly homemade and apprentice-trained craftsmen's furniture, at first only the barest essentials, did perhaps still cushion and somewhat brighten the utter weariness of trying "t' git along" on the frontiers.

Broadleafed contrasting shades of greenery on countless species — oak, ash, beech, walnut, maple, cherry, chestnut and elm, to name a few — were suddenly interrupted by darker "stands" of pineywoods (mostly evergreen) keeping watch above all. Those were the impressive guardians of the forests, many pines reaching incredible heights of a 100 to 125' and beyond, while diameters could measure at least five feet. Eventually, the conifers (cone-bearing) furnished more timber than any other of our native trees.

Reams have been written about pines, of their generosity to mankind, offering resin, pitch, turpentine, pulp for paper, timbers, even needles and cones. But herein our concern is the furniture built from their lumber. Some artifacts labeled "pine" are actually a combination of one or more different woods. This could have been original planning by the makers, or perhaps they "ran out of" primary material and ended up using whatever else suitable was at hand, from local preferences, or maybe they just changed their minds as they worked along. Too, contrasting characteristics of other woods might have been desired for certain appearances, extended rigidities, veneerings, etc.

For reference expediency, lumbermen divided all trees into hardwoods and softwoods, with pines further classified white (its cone and tassel the emblem of Maine), yellow and red. Both hardwoods and softwoods, once so plentiful during New England's early days, grew in some family variety over most of our country. There were, among innumerable others, the Ponderosa, Monterey, Pitch, the huge-coned Sugar Pine, the flaky-thick-barked Loblolly, and the valuable Georgia, so-called Southern Yellow Pine in those appropriate areas.

First used for a secondary wood (drawer backs and bottoms, for instance), pine graduated to full-piece furniture status when its excellent qualities became recognized. In great demand, hardwood Southern Yellow Pine far outranked white and red. In floorboards, massive lids on chests, trunks, thick tabletops and framings — it had no problem with that continuous energetic wear. Soft white surpassed hard as soon as it was known that when properly cured (air dried), it had the longevity and strength of oak. Remarkably free of knots, its straight, smooth grain readily lent itself to graceful curves,

carvings, moldings, extensively sought for wainscoting.

Heartpine, presently in high favor, means wood from the heart of a (huge diameter) pine tree. It is straight grained and without knots in white pine and fine grained in yellow. This choice portion could be milled into wide one-board furniture sections. Disappearing from overall deforestation (overcutting) of our virgin timberlands, heartpine is no longer available (except a few that undoubtedly remain in national preserves) because younger growths haven't had eons in which to reach parental dimensions. So we now find entirely or partially heartpine furniture objects highly valued, and they don't remain unsold in dealers' outlets for very long.

Natural finishes, painting, stenciling, paint-graining and such were smoothly applied. In the 1600's, paint tints were usually greens, blacks, reds (barn, Indian, turkey wattle, brick) and pumpkin (mustard) yellows, followed into the 1700's by additional soft grayish-blues adorning walls and wainscotings. A popular color on wagon wheels, indigo plant dyes were thus "wagon wheel blues". Each family, as did the craftsmen, had their own special paint "receipts," texture and depth of colors dependent upon local natural resources. There were yellow, red or gray clays (as found and used by the Egyptians thousands of years ago). Charcoal was used in blacks, dogwood berries for one of the greens. Roots were dug, stems, flowers and leaves were steeped, barks of trees and walnuts were boiled, milk and buttermilk scalded for casein bases, while even the chickens cooperated giving egg yolks for blending and egg whites for binders. Increasingly, collectors enjoy pine pieces bearing original paint, or at least "traces of." (There's something touchingly appealing about it.) Surges of popularity occur among all furniture woods, but year in and year out, pine seems to hold its own; briefly displayed, it is soon claimed by intrigued shoppers.

By the 1700's, craftsmen were using wood joinings similar to our 20th century types, the difference being they expended interminably painstaking hours fashioning artifacts with handtools; builders now have mechanical assistance and good electric lights "to see by." Early butt joints could warp — and usually did — large and small varying types of mortise and tenon took care of that. Very old lap joints (first spelled and called "rebate" — now generally "rabbet") were improved and replaced by tongue and groove joints (a standout rib in the side of one board fitted into a matching slot cut into another board) for a flush (smooth) look, actually a sort of stretched-out mortise and tenon. Another kind of mortise and tenon called "dovetailing" in wide usage — for corners of boxes and drawers, for instance — a fanned-out bird's tail, was most secure. Primitive two- or three-unit dovetails (one or two tails with thick pins, some looking crudely whittled out) gradually went on to finer four, five, and more units. The rounded dovetailings seen mostly in straight lines, albeit attractive, were factory produced. With so much latitude in wood joinings, makers could express individual ideas to the point that for some years long nails were seldom, if ever, necessary.

Pine furniture abided contentedly through generations in rural communities with few or no changes at all. Never pretentious, it didn't try to compete with elegancies keeping pace with the more formal life-styles in the cities. Sometimes country makers did try to incorporate a small degree of sophistication, but the pieces lacked that ultimate refinement of lines, still retaining a kind of hominess. Plain or sorta-fancy, pine furniture can sit comfortably and confidently among beautiful period pieces in today's homes, feeling not at all like country mice.

In checking over a chest of drawers, an elusive almost-imagined whiff of scent might escape from the raw pinewood back of a long-closed drawer, mindful of remote pine fragrances once drifting over quietly-soothing forest trails.

Since colonial times, pine furniture has held — and will continue to hold — its own distinctively respected place in our heritage simply by being itself.

A Home Restored

Originally built in 1861 by a family for whom an adjacent town on the shores of Lake Ontario in northwestern New York State had been named, this rural home was restored for 20th century occupancy with few structural changes. Pine had been used for all interior wood, and so it remained. Most refurbishing efforts were restricted to cleaning and refreshing the old pine boards. The painted surfaces had been submerged for generations under coats of browns, mustards and eggplant, colors influenced by then-current trends. Removal took 40 gallons of stripper.

Note fieldstones and concrete
lintels over the windows.

Interior view of the home with all original pine
furniture. Wouldn't the first owners have enjoyed that air conditioner.

Walls 19" thick made very deep window embrasures, seats for dreaming out upon gardens and fields beyond, or wide shelves for family treasures (along with the practical effect of insulation).

Document Box
ca. mid-1800's
L.12", H.8", Depth, 8"
Curved one-piece top with narrow band each side fitting over the box; original key is missing; square nails; brass carrying handle. Soft pine corners are worn round and the box has that special age-patina impossible to adequately copy on imitations.

Pegged natural pine floors, 6" to 7" width boards, were sanded and refinished. Termites' tracks are an interesting feature.

Pine trees which are eventually used in furniture.

Upstairs Bedroom Door
White painted, notice the original doorknobs and fittings.

Back Door of the Home
Heartpine, random width boards 6" to 8½, overall height 79¾", W.42". Original handforged iron hardware — two strap hinges L.31", 3½" widest part.

Bathtub and Beds

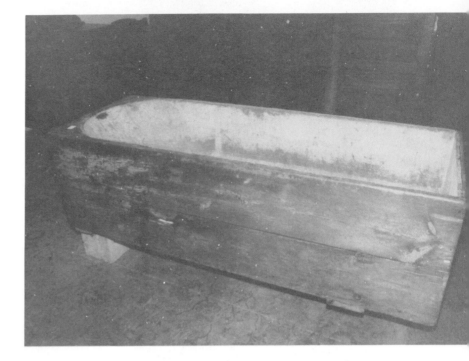

Bathtub
ca. 1800's
L.96", W.25¾", Depth 19".

Copper liner rounded at one end; drainage hole; mounted on wood blocks for sales display only — sits flat on the floor.

Child's Bed
Slats held "ticking" cloth mattress in place; half-side sloping arms at the top end continuing onto lower side rails helped secure the small one from rolling out.

Once upon a long time ago, typical of many New England farm kitchens was the "Turnup Bed," a strong wooden frame that was hinge-fastened to a wall at the top. By night the foot of the bed rested on two very heavy wooden legs (folding type); by day the frame, complete with its bedding, was hooked by foot to the wall, then covered with homespun curtains or with doors. This was the sleeping place of the master and mistress (and children when they were ill and required constant looking after), chosen because the kitchen was the warmest (or the only heated) room in their home.

Bed
ca: 1800's
Back H.49½", baseboard H.33", W.51½", L.7", 15" wide pediment.
Oak and chestnut with pine; decorative heavy moldings and carved pediment.

Close-up of decorative moldings and carved pediment on bed

High Post Bed
Ca. 1850
L.87¾", W.64", roping 23½" from the floor; posts
H.72".
American pine and maple with extended head-
board.

With their low ceilings and one-room fireplace-
heated living spaces, American settlers first built
simple low wood bed frames, "beneath the eaves"
beds. Lacing or roping (rawhide seen in the South-
west), attached to knobs (pegs) or woven through
frame holes held some type of mattress — even
ticking stuffed with cornshucks. Though some lacing was still being used in early 1900, by 1860
they had been almost entirely replaced with wood
slats. Beds began changing around 1820, spurred
on by improved living conditions (and incomes),

Bedroom Commode
Ca. 1800's
H.32", W.29", Depth 17½".
Drawer and door both have wood knobs; lift
top with a deep well; the door opens into a
storage compartment that is divided by the
wood base of the well; molded scallop-edge
lid.

Benches and Stools

Settle
ca. 1800's
W.59", back H.38½" from seat almost 15"
deep; backboards vary from 1" to about
1½" wide; gracefully carved armrest sides
13" deep at their widest point.

These were especially favored by New England settlers in the 1600's and 1700's (fewer built in the 1800's). They sat squashed together on these benches pulled close to fireside during bitterly cold winters. Some settles were hooded, some were built to the floor, as here, to help ward off drafts. Many were painted, red most common. Too, seats might act as lifttops for concealed storage space, or there could be drawers below. Lap-and-leg coverlets might be thus conveniently handy, the space even being able to serve as a woodbox. (There were many variations stemming from this basic style bench — for one, with a lower back shaped as a table top, able to be tipped forward to serve, and with storage space under the seat. It would then be known as a Settle Table, Hutch Bench or Table.)

Mammy Bench — a Windsor variant Southern name for this piece, it was also known as the Mammy Chair, Mammy Rocking Settee, Cradle Settee, now generally called the bench.
ca. 1800-1820
It was purchased in Niagara County, New York, though probably not made there.
H.30", L.49½", W.17", 2" thick seat 14" from the floor.
(Note rocker replacement.)
It has the typically-Windsor uneven number of spindles — 17; notice the graceful curve-shaping of the arms and the solid wood removable gate with ba finials on the posts; when baby was being rocked behind the barrier, one of the sitter's feet idly moving back an forth on the floor to keep the rockers moving, hands could be freed for needlework; with the gate removed, th furniture became a bench which could seat several adults.

Surrey Seat
ca. latter 1800's
H.33", W.33", seat Depth 17", H.17" from the floor W.27½".
Of the 23 round spindles, one was broken off through the years and left "as is." Button upholstering to the origina black leather was restored and side runners added t prevent tipping.

Surrey Seat
ca. 1880-1890
Found in Tennessee
Seat W.33", Depth 14", H.18½;" overall H. 31".
Separate backrest placed on bentwood,
holding some tops of the 17 turned
spindles anchored at base in the back of the seat; was originally upholstered. Round iron firming fastened 7"
toward center each side of the seat's front edge continuing around and above bentwood arms fastened 5" length each
side of the top edge of the seat; squared tapered legs have been added for present practical bench usage.

Bench
ca.1860
Seat 48"L., H.18", Depth 14½"; high back 15"H. 18" rounded legs splayed
for added steadiness; 2 urn-shaped side splats rather than one at center, the
shaping typically Pennsylvania Dutch, its place of origin; gracefully designed
stayrail.

Advertising Bench
ca. early 1900's
L.54", H.15½", W.12¾".
Mid-western origin; dark stained pine with lightly faded pumpkin yellow original lettering; about 1" each side top overhang with four edges beveled; when discarded as a sign, it was made into a bench or coffee table with the addition of a well-crafted pine base. (While not advocating drastically changing original appearances or intent in usage of any old artifact beyond necessary repairs, here the transition seems conversationally practical.)

Bench
ca. 1800's
L.48", H.19", Depth 9½".
Originally black, painted yellowish brown at some time later; deep apron and stretcher each side; seat corners thoughtfully curved; handmade.

Bench
ca. 1880's
Extra long, German pine; made from an old bed; half-heart carved bracket foot sides mortised into seat. Usually a bit shorter than this one (and less cumbersome to handle), benches were often carried outside on pleasant days for "settin' down work" as shelling peas, stringing beans, washing berries, etc., less tiresome chores that didn't need "standin' up fer."

Milking Stool (Slab Seat)
ca. 1880's
H.10", L.10½", W.5½".
Early farm made; seat 1¾" thick; three splayed legs.

Work Bench
ca. 1800's
H.26", W.25", Depth 15".
Primitively homemade in Lancaster County, Penn.; One shelf and wide side-shaped aprons; made to last.

Stool
Virginia pine; H.19½", L.11½".
Dark stained; curved one-board each side.

Round Top Stool
ca. 1800's
H.21¼", seat dia. 11½".
Pine with legs carefully shaped in a mill or shop;
seat for a lower desk; splayed legs have two stretchers each of four sides.

Stool
H.24¼", 11½" square top.
A sturdy stool with square legs and stretchers joined with a crosspiece, the latter often used as a footrest.

Bins and Boxes

In early cabins of American Pioneers there was little time left from hunting and planting to build other than the most basic articles of furniture — and little space to fit them in. Could we ask one of those settlers what pieces he HAD to give his family, he might have said, "Waaaal, beds, tables, stools, benches, shelves — and don't forget the boxes — if we didn't have those to keep things in, the critters would carry us out bag and baggage. We kept them handy for my pipes, herbs, sugar if we had any, candles, spices, salt, saleratus (soda), bread, the shed grains, all kinds of food, our clothes not hanging up on wall pegs, ... and the woman's quilts." It wouldn't have occurred to him to differentiate into modern categories as "furnishings" and "accessories" — they were all fittings, one complementing the other. Boxes hung on walls, were set on tables and ledges, and made with or without lids in innumerable shapes and sizes. When those on walls became stuffed so full that nails or pegs would no longer hold them, they became floor pieces — eventually with drawers and legs. (He didn't mention chairs — they were mighty scarce on frontiers.)

Grain Box (or Bin)
ca. 1850
H.28" at back; 25" at front; L.79", Depth 28".
Three different sized lids slant down from a 9½" wide flat strip at top rear to which six hinges fasten. Finger-lifted, these covers open to three divided inside bins. An off-center and a corner-gnawed rathole gave unwelcome entry to critters. Northwestern New York State origin.

Meal Bin
ca. 1840-1850
Legs full sides; inside double bins retain age-dimmed and usage-lightly scarred pale blue paint which may have been added after the original date of making.

Open meal bin showing the inside double bins.

Meal Bin
ca. 1916
H.31", W.47", Depth 16".
Iron hinges; two inside bins divided to hold flour and (corn) meal. Handmade "on the place" at McMinnville, Tennessee by a very gentle man as a gift to his wife. The only time his children ever saw him display anger, he became so irate he kicked this bin!

That same husband whittled out this palette so his wife could more easily scoop its contents from the bin. 12" x 6" with a thumb and fingers hold; white pine.

Store Coffee Bin
ca. 1800's
H.32½", top board to which one side of the lid hinges are fastened is 7¾" wide, making a nice ledge; thick pine frame is ¾". Darkstained; slantfront lid lifts with wood knob; sharp edges of front, back, and both sides interior tin lining are well protected with a folded metal band at the top edges of the box; while pine and tin are both in very good condition, original painted lettering is indistinct, but enough to show it was put there.

Interior of store coffee bin.

Document Box
L.19", H.4½", W.5¾".
Hinged lid folds twice over; chamfered top lid; the hook and eye replace original key and key keeper; inner divided sections; Indiana origin.

Open document box showing chamfered top lid.

Dough Box
ca. 1840-1850
H.35½", W.35", Depth 18½".
An unusual hinged foldback top that forms a shelf for utensils, protected by a three-side gallery — certainly convenient; the foldback also exposes a wide hinged-to-lift flat pastry rolling or other work surface. Under that is a deep inside storage compartment; uncommon piece.

Dough box foldback open to show the work surface.

Dough Box
ca. 1800's
H.28½", W.19", L.32", Box 11" deep.
Pennsylvania made by hand; old red paint no longer completely hiding the traces of the original blue; wide five-board construction; round cutout circle unusual; carved halfround each side at middle, and soft curve (rather than sharper bracket-cut bases), are the features on each of the one-board sides in the Pennsylvania manner; it had no lid.

Dough Box
Slant lid opens on two iron hinges; legs tapered to top of box; Florida origin.

Dough Box
ca. 1850
H.27¾, W.42¾", Lid depth 21½", base W.31".
Pine and poplar. Sliding type lid; turned and grooved legs; wide apron; slanted out sides of a deep interior; dough was kneaded on the wide top.

Utility Box
ca. 1800's
Six-board construction; dovetailed four corners; start of a small damage or
gnawing on the front of the lid no deterrent.

Dutch or Amish Type Box
ca. 1800's
L.30½", W.13¾".
Pennsylvania origin in the original; 5" deep slanted up and out sides from a two-board bottom; the Dutch
sometimes put folded dry linens into these. They had a multitude of purposes. Present owner purchased to
hang under cove-covered light in her kitchen, first having it painted in the Pennsylvania style with bright fruit
and flower clusters; Mistress Pig wearing her pleasant look and her mobcap on her head (full crown and tied
under her chin) is bound to bring a "Good Morning" smile in return.

Utility (Catchall) Box
H.6½", L.13½", Depth 6¾".
Pine painted blue over mustard; square nails; originally had a type of wire lifts (marks seen) at each side to raise the lid.

Candle Box (Carrier)
L.14", H.3", W.6".
Nailed corners; thick wood; top-rounded carrying handle; unusual type of candle box but to the maker's idea; made "on the place" in Kentucky.

Salt Box
ca. 1790's
H.3¾". L.10", W.5", 9"H. at center divider carrie
Louisiana heartpine; handcarved.

Toolbox
H.11", L.34", W.9".
Refinished for holding today's household utensils; center-whittled thinner
for more comfortable hand carrying; center divider; handle mortised into
raised end pieces. Homemade in Ohio.

Wood Box
ca.1800's
H.28", L.21¾", W.15¾.
Northwestern New York State made; from 1" thick old beehive boxes; tin patches reinforce soft pine worn corners, typically and frugally "making do" with materials at hand; homemade.

Store Box
ca. 1800's—early 1900's
Origin of usage — Nashville, Tenn., for shipping Maxwell House Coffee; the containers usually placed on store floors for measuring out customers' orders; holds 100 lbs.; wire type hinges; an original paper label in fine condition increased the value; note the curlicue trims.

Store Shipping & Displaying Box
A good example, also showing popular soap bars for laundry "in those days."

Grandpa's Wonder Soap
H.8¼", L. 12¾", W.9".
26 dovetails each corner. Painted trademark design in black.

"Grandpa" has colonial-style curly long hair, his eyeglasses pushed up over his forehead, and beams at us with a wide smile.

Store Shipping & Display Boxes
Again — good old ones with their eminently desirable original paper labels; dovetailed four corners. "Ardent" Brand Cinnamon; elaborately designed label with packer given as W. G. Dean & Son, New York, and cinnamon called "Absolutely Pure"; slide lid. Southern Special Apples from Oregon; box 7⅝" high; had a nailed-on lid. These boxes are in intensely popular demand for all sorts of modern usages. Some acquire new lids, usually newly hinged-on.

Store Box
ca. latter 1800's-1900
Dovetailed four corners; original labels on outside of box and on the inside of the lid — Deininger Bros. Superior Biscuits; lift top — held with heavy wire hooks, evidence of an earlier opening thumb lift.

Strongbox
ca. 1800-1810
H.10", L.19", Depth 11".
Extended lid; handforged iron fixtures; swing-aside brass keyhole cover (with no key) has a stamped eagle's head, (looks like — age worn dim), the stamping similar to those found on buttons of the 1790-1820 era; base end of the hinged clasp, held under the lid by a top lid cluster of three decorative half-buttons, locks into the long lock slot on the keyplate. So carefully and pridefully hand fashioned, this container may have held paper currency, gold coins or vital documents.

Travel Box
ca. 1800's-early 1900
Dome topped; strap iron bound lid (to strengthen against bumps) opens on
hinges to a deep well with a top liftout tray; brass button decor; iron keeper
now has no key; iron bound four corners; original finish; leather handles.

Utility Box
H.1½", W.8", L.24¾".
Handmade during the 1800's with dovetailed corners,
this plain little box served well for a long time for many
usages, one could have been gathering long stemmed
flowers and herbs for home medicine cures and potpouri;
skunk cabbage might have been carried in it for making
green dyes.

Cabinets and Cupboards

**Hotel Mail Cabinet
ca. 1880-1890
H.6'33", W.14".
Six shelves having 36 individual guest mail sections; short bracket feet base; original key missing; double solid doors.**

Open Hotel mail cabinet showing the individual guest mail sections.

Baker's Cabinet (Kitchen)
ca. 1900
Height at top 30", at base 30", W.47¾".
Top drawers with porcelain knobs, lower and cradle bottom compartments were brass handles; top door storage; straight and turned legs, the squared upper part extending to the top of the lower drawers as side posts.

Tool Cabinet (Chest)
ca. 1800's
W.18½", Depth 10½". Thick wood top; dividers inside the three drawers; thick wood top; finely crafted.

Doll's Cabinet
H.24½", W.12" widest part, Depth 6".
Homemade, painted blue pine; wood knobs; one inside shelf; three-board back is tongue and grooved.

Fruit Drying Cabinet (also for corn, herbs, and flower petals, etc.)
ca. 1800's
H.25½", L.18½," W.14½".
Amish origin; sheet metal base H.8", L.20", holds the detachable (liftoff) cabinet of drawers. (Originally there was no top so the owner added this thick wooden one for practical purposes.)

Open fruit drying cabinet which is now used in a home for drying rose petals and other flowers for potpourri fragrances (lavender a long-time universal favorite); eight drawers, the four corners of each mortised and tenoned together, each drawer bottom coarsely screened; iron pull knobs; the back has a firming iron crosspiece brace diagonally from each top corner to the opposite bottom one; slices of fruit, etc. were laid on the screens and the whole on the iron base set on top of a stove, kept from burning by the dryer's iron base touching the hot surface, and drying the drawers' fresh contents. Can't you just smell the delicious odors emanating from the rack?)

Cabinet
ca. 1800's
H.67½", W.47"
Shoefoot base; combined woods with pine; random width pine boards at back; dark stained; the pine is called Spanish pine; knotholes; original iron hinges; eight front panels, each have nine shaped spindles that ventilate the cabinet; at the sides are four panels, each having seven spindles about 11" high; inside are four shelves; this is an unusual cabinet, described as suitable for a food safe or even a bookcase. Seen at a mall in Orange Park, Fla.

**Kitchen Cabinet
ca. 1800's
Made in two lift-off sections; base H.30⅞" W.42",
Depth 16½". Two shelves; top with glass doors
is H.37",
W.37½", Depth 12".**

This kitchen cabinet was found in Tennessee and
also has two shelves behind the glass doors; brass
fixtures with butterfly hinges; handfashioned and
all original.

Kitchen Pie/Food Safe ca. 1850-1860
H.46", W.40½", one-board top W.17", sides each one-board W.16".
Handmade at St. Augustine, Florida.
Two drawers with dovetail corners and selfwood knobs; finely woven screens fill in two 5¼" diameter cut-out round holes for insect-deterrent ventilation; three inside shelves; a whittled turn latch holds the two doors; there is a slight no-harm mark probably left by an original latch just above a whittled-out keyhole (now without the key) so the safe could have been locked, somewhat uncommon on this type of furniture.

Milk and Food Safe (Kitchen Cabinet)
H.46", W.38½", Depth 21".
Heartpine; original green paint now still softly apparent; two inside shelves; common black screen fills in ventilating and bug-deterrent side-front panels; a knife-cut pivot latch keeps the wide door closed where once there was an original catch of some sort.

Side of a Food Safe
This looks as though the extra piece may have been set on when the original screening became torn or rusted; a heartpine piece is the bottom strengthening addition. (The damage at the side is a little high for a gnawing unless the furniture was set against a piece high enough to convenience the critter.)

Pie Safe (Kitchen Cabinet Also Used For Bread and
Meat Storage)
ca. 1850-1860
H.53", W.38½", Depth 17".
With today's demand for these pieces, they are now
kept in rooms other than a kitchen; were principally
made in the American mid and far west; sometimes
seen with pierced tin side panels although front only
were made in greater numbers; all intended to keep
out rodents and insects, afford ventilation for foods
stored inside, and to make this essential furniture
more attractive.

Pie Safe
ca. 1800's
H.59¼, W.37½", Depth 14½".
Straight legs are most seen on old kitchen furniture;
three inside shelves here, a long drawer at the
bottom, porcelain knobs; tins pierced from the
outside makes a smooth exterior, the finest quality
type; the piercing, width and type of boards and
overall construction skills are considered in evalu-
ations.

Food Safe
ca. 1800's
H.63", W.33", one-board top Depth 17".
Three deep shelves; coarse screening on top half of each of the two tall front doors; glass pulls and a top whittled pivot latch to hold the doors closed; sides are solid pine panels.

Food (Pie) Safe
ca. 1800's
H.57½", W.31", Depth 15½". White painted; three shelves; top drawer groove trimmed; the white was put on over original green paint; the old screening is gone. Marked for display only, but an evaluation for a similar piece is given in the index.

Pie (Kitchen, Food, Milk) Safe
ca. 1800's
H.66½", W.33½", Depth 18¾".
Fine screening at front, one side panel is screened, the other side is a solid pine panel (screen probably was torn, and they decided wood would be better); slide (sideways) iron latches; this type holds the doors, and they don't need the extra whittled latch at the top or bottom; the long legs are "coltish" and attractive — and kept the rodents out.

Food Safe
ca. 1800's
H.58", W.39½", Depth 16".
Knotty pine and oak; refinished; fine screening on six panels; three shelves; the sides and back are solid pine, the inside recently painted a soft bright blue; new porcelain knobs have center clusters of blue flowers; narrow full width drawer; an iron top pivot latch holds the doors closed; there is a large (original) rat hole at one corner of the bottom shelf; side panels each have a 1½" wide reinforcing pine strip.

"Hoosier" Cabinet
ca. after 1900
Built in two sections; work table 31" from the floor, W.47½", Depth 27"; top H.40", W.38", Depth 12¾"; 11" wide boards each side. Brass knob on pullout breadboard; glass knobs on two drawers and one on the right of two glass wood-framed doors where also is seen a whittled latch on the opposite doorside; white centered metal handles on the "possum belly" bentwood lower bins. (In addition to the breadboard, factories often advertised these cabinets with "built-in flour bins and sifters" — sometimes even a coffee grinder.

"Pop Bottle" Cooling Cabinet
ca. latter 1800's
Tongue and grooved legs and sides; iron handgrips and hinges on two lift-up tops covering tin-lined interior deep well; still operational; the Dealer suggests using this as a coffee table, without changing the original appearance.

Kitchen Cabinet
ca. 1800's
H.48½, W.56" base; workshelf Depth 23½".
Pine-oak-walnut combination woods. Made from the top of an old bed with apple crates for drawers, soda boxes for their sides; one bottom drawer tongue and grooved as well as the fronts of the top doors, the latter with pull knobs and center whittled pivot latches; fancifully molded pediment (ornamental top of a cased piece).

Medicine Cabinet
ca. 1900
H.25½", W.21½", Depth 4⅞".
Original glass, shelves inside painted white, brass hardware.

Store Cabinet
ca. 1800's
H.84", W.46", Depth 20" base, setback forms a shelf 8" deep.
Strong traces of bluish-white paint left in nailheads after piece was stripped; two shelves behind lower door and four shelves behind two top doors; porcelain knobs on slide closures of three doors; black iron drawer pulls have open spaces under which glass or cardboard paper labels could be inserted to denote contents of the particular drawer; decorative molding on top cornice. These flat-to-the-floor pieces were sometimes built flush with walls or as part of a cabinet unit; here it is the readily movable two sections.

Table and Storage Cabinet with door open to show storage space.

Table and Storage Cabinet
H.58", W.44", Depth 22½".
Southern yellow pine, traces of white paint still clinging to tongue and groove backing of one storage space; new porcelain knobs; plain black iron curved pull on drawer which is divided into two sections; grooved molding trim.

Store Spool Cabinet
H.11¾", W.24⅞", Depth 16¾", Top Overhang ¾".
Ash is the primary wood, pine is the secondary wood. Small mortise and tenon joinings; spool divider slots clearly marked inside the three drawers although wooden divider strips are gone (to have those originals adds to the value); self-wood knobs with one partially broken on the top drawer; outside corners are decoratively cut as pillars; pine used for insides of drawers; impressed lettering still very good.

Side view of the store spool cabinet. These are now greatly in demand, and this is a particularly fine example.

Closed Cupboard (Architectural Piece)
ca. 1850-1880
H.62½", W.40½", Depth 7½".
Washed white pine; original glass, self pull knobs, tongue and grooved back; five shelves with plate grooves; wide top cornice matches base (in reverse); this is an example of cupboards built in and flush with the walls of a (dining) room; sometimes the cornices and bases are a continuation of those decorating the room's walls.

Baker's Cupboard
ca. 1900-1910
H.70", Base H.28", Top H.42", Base Depth 26", Top Depth 14½", W.42".
Hoosier (Indiana) Amish origin. Made from packing crates from Cattaraugus Cutlery Company; chestnut drawer fronts; random width back boards; typical store-type metal fixtures, both pull and slide drawer and door openers; a lot of storage space with an extra-wide working surface; (mortar and pestle sit on small curved shelf, along with several butter prints).

Bread Board
ca. 1890
Tennessee origin.
Hole bored one end for wall hanging; set-on low rim each side slightly raised above board's surface to hold pastries being rolled within board limits.

Baker's Rack Drawer (Shelf)
L.24", W.17¾", gallery 3" deep.
Dovetailed four corners; cutout hand pullout slot one end; used for round bread "raising/rising," the whitened areas left where the damp dough was placed until ready for baking; fit into a rack with other shelves.

Closed Cupboard
ca. 1860
Overall H.79", Depth 21", W.62½", 6½" deep dry sink, stepback 8½", deep top molding W.4".
Bracket feet; four shelves behind top doors, two below; tongue and groove joined boards at back; two chamfered panels on each of four doors; the only new feature is the refinishing. First built in two portable sections, noted about 1350 as "Cuppeboardes" — shelves or boards to hold cups (and I suppose, occasionally, as now, suitably sized overflows from other places) — made in America about 300 years later — they grew along as storage units with, eventually, glass or solid wood doors. Still, usually, in two portable sections, they could be easily moved around — or — without feet, they were built into the walls themselves.

Open Cupboard
ca. 1870
H.60¼", W.36", Depth 19½", 3" deep cornice.
Southern pine from the Atlanta, Georgia area. Random width boards at back; iron fixtures.

Closed Cupboard (Show and Store)
H.79", W.62¼", Depth 21", stepback 8½"; 4" deep molded top cornice.
Original solid wood doors were replaced with glass in the original wood framing; those and original solid wood doors below all have iron fixtures; four shelves above and two below; tongue and grooved back.

Closed Cupboard (Flat Back)
ca. 1850
H.76", W.42½".
All original; four paneled doors with darker wood pivot latches; three inside shelves above and two below.

Closed Cabinet
ca. mid-1800's
W.39", one-board sides each W.16½".
Heartpine-Mississippi origin. Three shelves; bracket
feet on full height boards; whittled turn latch; coving
overhang.

Closed Cupboard
ca. 1810-1820
H.60", W.54",
One-board each side. Three shelves; Alabama heartpine; pegged construction; grooved wide cornice; whittled pivot latch.

Closed Cupboard opened to show the three shelves.

Closed Cupboard (Sideboard, Dining Server)
ca. 1840
H.42", W.56", Depth 21", pointed gallery H.8½".
Empire S-roll front drawers dovetailed; self knobs; three doors open into three separate storage units with two shelv
each; octagonally cut posts on front sides; short turned ball feet; the glowing primary pine wood was refinished af
being stripped of its original age-scarred and flaking mahogany veneering.

In the 1400's, "side boards" were cloth-covered steps, as many as nine in great halls of estates, the top shelf reserved for utensils for serving royalty, the other steps holding dinner wares and potteries. In (one-room) keeping rooms of more humble cabins and cottages there were fewer steps, but everywhere always kept at the room sides. As years went by, flat boards were placed with ends on the steps, holding foods for serving; the steps became cabinets, flat top tables appeared, and soon with the continuing addition of many storage compartments, gradually came the massive sideboards. In America, white or yellow pine woods were principally used from New England into Virginia and throughout Maryland. Southern pieces were light cabinets on legs with table tops, known as "Hunt Boards." Never typically "country pieces," with a few exceptions, sideboards became highly popular during the latter 1800's reign of the "Golden Oak," built with many variations in style, but generally those with which we are now most familiar.

Closed Cupboard (Kitchen)
ca. mid-1800's
H.31½", W.31½", Depth 17".
Three board back continuing above display/working surface of cupboard 3½"; completely handfashioned — note that one of the two wood knobs was put on out of line with the other; whittled wood pivot latches below the knobs and a one-board flat work surface.

Closed Cupboard
ca. 1880
H.32", W.29", Depth 17".
New England white pine; two-board overhang top; three inside shelves; ornamental brass knob and key keeper.

Corner Wardrobe (Cupboard)
ca. 1890
H.78"-80", W.54", 9" deep sides.
English pine; has one key; brass pull knob; grooved wide cornice; inside shelf near top; the narrow scalloped base had to be replaced; tongue and groove joinings; refinished.

Corner Wardrobe opened to show inside shelf.

Corner Cupboard
ca. 1800-1820
H.61½", 37½" across open front, side panels each
W.5½", four shelves each 15½" depth, sides back to
22¼".
**Right out of early south Alabama; original painted
pine, gray inside and green outside; after being
refinished to natural, traces of the two original
colors remain.**

Corner Cupboard
ca.1850
H.7'2", front opening W.29", sides adjoining the back
"V" each 20".
**Handsomely crafted with scallop edged shelves and
base; decorative cornice; brass ring pull to open base
revealing inside shelves.**

Jelly (Kitchen) Cupboard
H.31", W.15", L.37½".
An early one; natural pine handmade; two inside shelves; one-board top; single door with iron hinges and a porcelain knob.

Kitchen Safe (Cupboard)
ca. 1910
H.37½", W.24", Depth 10½".
"Back yard" project made by hand; two-board door; heavy traces of original white paint; square iron hinges; one-board sides with bootjack legs; Florida origin.

Closed Cupboard (Kitchen Safe) ca. early 1800's
Base L.36", W.31½", Depth 18"
Gallery L.37½", W.20½, Depth 3".
Thoughtfully handcrafted rarity; all original; uncommon slide latch governs operation of a porcelain knob; rare corner treatment where the three-side gallery covers the front corners; two inside shelves; found near Ransomville, NY.

Side view of closed cupboard showing rare corner treatment.

Open Cupboard
H.70", Depth 18½", W.36½".
Originally painted green with traces left; tongue and grooved three-panel door with a
brass turn latch; two inside shelves; iron hinges.

Pewter Cupboard (Open Cupboard/Desk)
ca. 1830
H.6'3½", W.34", Depth 15¾".
Handmade and used in a North Carolina Tavern for many years — and while it probably was not made as a "pewter cupboard," pewter ware for serving customers was kept in both the open and closed sections. From this custom the innkeepers always called it their "pewter cupboard," as it is still known today. It's aptly termed since there was a scarcity of china and pottery which was more expensive, and pewter didn't break. (The term is today applied to many open cupboards as it was back then.) This cupboard has handforged and hand-hammered squarehead nails and shanks (shanks the part below the nailhead); breadboard overhang top; and four open display shelves. A fallfront conceals 10 irregularly sized cubbyholes and a flat surface for writing (and figuring); one door has whittled turnlatch and encloses more storage shelves; very short bracket feet are part of the cabinet's vertical boards.

Chairs

Armchair, Shaker Slat-Back
ca. 1840 (could be earlier)
H.34", W. arm to arm 23", seat 17" from floor.
Pine in combination with chestnut, maple and cherry arms; three shaped slats narrowed at the ends to fit into the stiles (side uprights); tapered bottom of uprights at the floor; typical Shaker "Scroll Arms," or as termed by them, "Ladle Arms." The hole in the right arm caused by the sitter resting her spindle there as she worked could only have been achieved after many years of this habit. Seat has been replaced. (Shakers' three-slat chairs are thought to have originated with the New York family branch of New Lebanon known as the "Brickyard" or "East Family"; as with all Shaker furniture, this provides a lightness and perfection of workmanship.

Folding Chair
ca. 1800's-early 1900's
All pine in slats and wider boards; iron bolted; made and stamped under one armrest by the manufacturer "Parks Mfg. Co., South Paris, Maine, USA." This company made fine quality children's sleds and wheelbarrows for many years.

"Country" Rocking Chair
ca. early 1800's
H.39", Seat 16" from floor, 19½" wide and 16½" deep.
Green painted; restored seat; three plain slats; note finials at the top of the leg posts; similarly flat cut at the tops of the stiles of the back.

Rocking Chair
ca. 1800's
H.34½", seat 15" from floor; widest part 16½".
Restored seat; these finials indicate an early 1800's construction; shaped stayrail and two
plain slats; combined pine and maple; Shaker style.

Slat-Back Rocking Chair
ca. 1810-1820
H.30¾", Seat 14" from floor, 15" wide at front and
12" at the back.
Three shaped slats on curved back uprights; chair
all original; painted brick red with black striping
trim.

Side view of slat-back rocking chair showing the
heavy woven cord seat beginning to fray.

Arrowback Windsor Side Chair
ca. 1800-1820
H.31¾", seat is 18¼" from the floor, W.16", 16¾"
deep and 1¾" thick.
New England origin; original black finish (black
sometimes painted over deliberate red); "Donkey
Ears" (or "Rabbit Ears") are the flattened tops of
the side uprights — they curve widely back in a style
of Hitchcock and more accented with Sheraton —
supporting a deeply incurved top stayrail (headpiece); four arrowhead spindles are curved with the
side posts; saddleseat slope; stamped on the seat's
underside is "Maker B. Klein."

Side view of Arrowback Windsor Side Chair; note
the front stretcher is also arrow-shaped at center.

Low Kitchen Chair
ca. 1800's
H.32", Seat 17" wide, Depth 15".
Actually, with a number of uses in each family, these low chairs were called by whatever task they most "sat for" — churning, for one — for ladies putting on their slippers for another — even in a pinch toted out and set in the "wagain" (now spelled and pronounced "wagon") for still another seat, although the shaped headpiece and two slats are shaped more than those seen in wagon chairs. Low stretchers indicate chair may have started out a bit taller, then been cut off as the bottoms of the legs wore beyond redemption.

Country Kitchen Chair
ca. 1850's
H.32¾", seat 14½" at widest part, depth 15".
Four plain turned spindles with round sideposts; comfortably shaped seat distantly related to a saddle seat; one of a set of four; seen in Tennessee.

Rod-Back Side Chairs
ca. 1800's, Windsor
H.44", seat 17½" from floor, 15" deep, 14" at widest part of the back.
Thick pine seat without knots hasn't been warped and for years has given comfortable sitting; slightly splayed legs; tops of the stiles and legs have been whittle-tapered at the ends; this sturdy purely-Provincial country style widespread in England from the latter 1700's into the turn of the 19th century was an idea carried here by American colonists; probably for color in bland lives and to disguise the fact that they used various woods in making them, chairs more often than not were painted. Today when we think of "country" atmospheres, we recognize these chairs.

Side Chair (as is)
ca. 1800's
H.33", seat depth 15", W.13½" to 14".
This probably was originally painted and stencilled, the decoratively center splat typical
of those seen 1825-1840's in Pennsylvania, combined woods with pine; one of a set of
four and being sold individually "as is" since the back is loose and it needs refinishing.
(no customary drill hole signs at front stretcher.)

Side Chair (Slat Back)
ca. 1800's
H.35", W.14"-16", Depth 13¾", seat 15¼" from floor.
Original button-top upright finials' worn almost flat from age and handling of the chair; new seat; front leg posts still holding but have split tops.

Side Chair (Straight Slat Back)
ca. 1800's
H.35", seat 10¾" deep, 10½" to 9" wide, 17" from floor.
What were originally heavy side post donkey ears are now badly worn; seat at some time replaced, still in pretty fair condition.

Rod-Back Windsor Highchair
ca. 1830-1840
H.35¼", seat H.23½" from the floor, seat W.12" and
Depth 11¾".
All original; briefly splayed legs so it won't easily tip
over; dark finish black over red with stencil flowers
on the typical wide headrest; the footrest has been
worn thin.

"Firehouse" Windsor Variant Youth Chair
H.31", W.13¾", Depth 13". Five back spindles, two
only a bit larger, acting as the top side posts; ¾" thick
wood back; footrest 2½" wide. Tennessee found.

Primitive Youth Chair
ca. 1800's
H.35", seat W. at front 15", 13½" at back.
At some time since the original making, the seat was
replaced; tapered bottom legs while the two at the
rear extend on to form the back uprights; these
could be pulled up to the table for an older child not
requiring a tray.

Child's Side Chair
ca. late 1800's-early 1900's
H.23", seat H.12½" from floor, 10¾" deep, W. at
seat back 9" to 10½", posts 12" apart at back;
English pine with oak, painted.

Chests

Apothecary Chest
ca. 1800's.
H.74", W.36", Depth 18½.
16 drawers, bottoms tin-lined; sizes graduated from half widths wider at the top, down to a two deeper full width drawers at the bottom; three chamfered panels on each chest side, those sides held together with wood pins; has been refinished to natural color.

Child's Chest of Drawers' ca. 1900
H.24½", W.17¾," Depth 8½".
Handfashioned as a gift; six drawers and nice wide top for "putting things on"; one-board back; porcelain pulls.

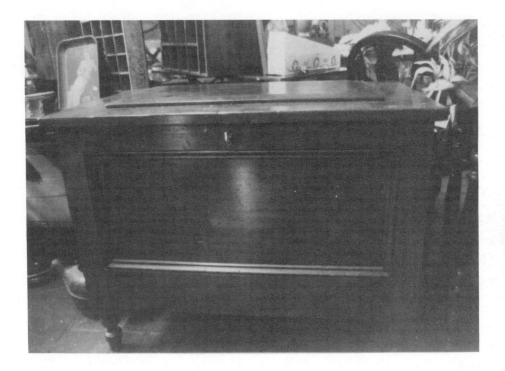

Blanket Chest
ca. 1870
H.28½", L.38", W.22½".
Cherry stained pine; cut in initials "F.A."; hand-forged concealed hinges; replacement key; chamfered top; turned feet; inside is a narrow one-side box for keepsakes — or could hold pine cones against moths, etc.

Blanket Chest
H.34½", W.38½", Depth 23½". Slant top; four corners dovetailed; iron hinged for liftup top; chubby double-ball turned feet.

Chest of Drawers (Bureau/Dresser)
ca. 1800's (Victorian era)
H.34¾", W.38", Depth 17½" base; from the bottom to top of mirror H.38½", top W.31" at its widest part.
Two small lift-top "handkerchief" drawers; four large walnut striped drawers with walnut stained fruit pulls; completely original pine wood feather grained finish; mercury tilting mirror; candle shelves at each side of mirror; crested molded pediment.

Two country pieces displayed together in a shop but valued separately.
Top: Multi-Drawer Chest of Chest of Drawers (Cabinet)
ca. 1800's (very old)
H.19½", W. 53", Depth 12½".
Nailed together; 12 drawers in various sizes; self knobs.

Bottom: Storage Cabinet (Closed Cabinet)
ca. 1880
H.35", W.73", Depth 13".
Bottom chest is old but the top one is much earlier. Replacement brass
knobs; common wire screening in four chamfered drawers (it could be for
storing items needing ventilation); two inside shelves; one side is tongue and
grooved, the other side is plain.

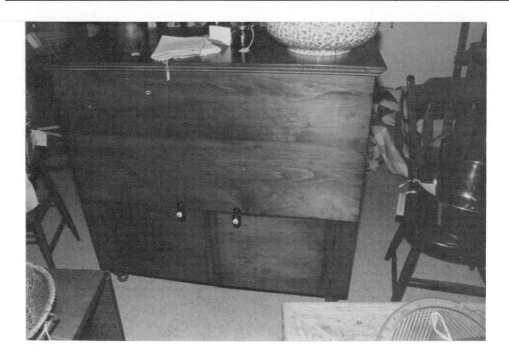

Flour Chest
ca. 1870
H.40", W.44", Depth 21½".
Lift top opening to a deep well; two iron-fixture porcelain-knobbed doors with inside storage ceilings that are the bottom of the well, thus dividing the storage areas; short small ball-turned feet; groove edged cornice-type small overhang on lift top.

Chest of Drawers
ca. 1860
H.31½" plus scallop-cut gallery H.9" at highest center one-board top W.35", Depth 17".
English pine stripped and waxed; three sides gallery atop and slightly inset from the molded top edge of the chest two long and two smaller drawers with self knobs; double ball low feet.

Chest of Drawers
ca. 1800's
H.48", W.46½", Depth 20".
Natural finish light pine; self knobs; five drawers
dovetailed at their four corners; short ball-turned
feet.

Chest of Drawers
ca. 1860-1870
H.36", W.33½", Depth 17½".
Each drawer dovetailed four corners; large porcelain pulls are replacements; all four drawers can be
locked but now no keys to do so; three sides shaped
gallery.

Chest of Drawers
ca. 1880
H.41", W.40", Depth 15¾", shaped back gallery H.4½"
Handmade; stripped and finished to wood tones, but traces of original paint still cling obstinately — they are difficult to entirely obliterate on most pieces; square nails used; five drawers once able to be locked now have missing keys; key keeper on one top drawer was restored but so well done it is scarcely noticeable; one-board each side W.14"; drawer sides and backs were made from scrap wood, as shipping crates or boxes.

Miniature Chest
H.14", W.19", Depth 5¾".
Beveled edge top one-board; black stained knobs. It could be a salesman's sample, but usually those are much more expensive, so this may be a child's.

Chest of Drawers
ca. 1840-1850
H.46", W.39½", Depth 17¼".
Handfashioned; found at Clarence, NY; plain grain walnut drawer front veneers on white pine with walnut-stained pine drawer pulls; two small shelves with low back gallery; gracefully scalloped valances at base are matched by those carved on bracketed feet of one-board sides; side edges of both flat ledges are walnut stained, effectively contrasting with the pine.

Store Chest
H.36", W.27¾", Depth 22".
Iron drawer pulls are typical of store furniture of this an
later periods, these dated on their undersides 1869
New Hampshire origin; mortised drawer corners.

Spice Chest
ca. 1700's-early 1800's
(It is difficult to precisely date this country furniture due
to unchanging styles for so many years, a great many
pieces being handfashioned at home or to the rural
makers' or customers' ideas.)
L.25", H.24", Depth 11½".
Originally found in a barn in northwestern New York, then
put into an auction where it was bought by the present
owners.

Tool Box (Chest)
ca. 1800's
H.18", L.34", Depth 19".
Well used but still in good condition despite some nicks; unpainted interior.
Outside has the original dark green paint now almost black with age.

Utility Chest (Cabinet)
(One dealer listed it as a Bucket Bench)
ca. 1800's
H.21¾", W.37½, Depth 15¼.
Variations of color shadings in the pine; six drawers with porcelain knobs.

Desks

Lift-Top (Bible Box) Desk
ca. 1850
L.24¾", Depth 20¾", H. at front 9½", 16" at back including the gallery.

Natural finish pine; two-board back, bottom is random width boards; nicely carved gallery protects objects that can be placed on the narrow top shelf; two concealed hinges hold slanting lift-top (writing surface on the lid) that hides interior cubbyholes and space for a Bible; handfashioned on the Niagara Frontier, the dealer displayed as a Bible Box, and this article does fit both categories in appearance and usage. During the 1700's such boxes began to acquire legs (or some type of frame bases), often simply set on stands or tables; (early example might have secret compartments for important papers, wills, and so on); on into the 1800's, the boxes kept growing into desk types more familiar to us now.

Mill Desk
ca. 1800's
H.45", W.36", Depth 23", 1¼" H. gallery at back.
Slanted lift-top; scalloped front additions are added supports as well as decoration; at the rear the two also hold a handy shelf; one inside compartment.

Plantation Desk
ca. 1800's
H.34½", W.32½", Depth 29"; solid doors on cabinet top H.24½", W.33½", Depth 17".
Selfwood whittled turn catches on doors and had a desk key; top cabinet shelves with two vertical dividers; these sections seen on other plantation desks to hold the slaves' registry books and other records; finely molded cornice, this making a top shelf; a Georgia piece.

Primitive Desk (Box)
ca. 1800's
H.12" at top, W. 20", Depth 24".
Georgia origin; low paper-hold bar; well used.

School Desk
ca. 1910-1920
H.32", W.21", Depth 32".
Two-piece folding parts; all pine frame with ten narrow and two wide boards forming seat and back; in a schoolroom row with one desk back of another, the seat at the front, as here, provides a seat for a pupil who uses, in turn, the desk of the unit in front of his, thus the desk/seat accommodates two children; made with little danger of tipping and has a large deep well under the desk surface for books, paper, pencils and such.

Side view of school desk.

School Desk
ca. 1800's
H.18½", W.18½", Depth 17¾".
A husky typically straight leg "country" style — dimensions properly scaled for small children; three-side gallery; iron hinges; lift top; surface is not too slanted for comfortably using as the work surface; hand made.

Front view of primitive school desk.

**School Desk (Primitive) Double for two pupils
ca. 1800's**
W.35", seat is 12½" from the floor, top 11¾" deep.
One board top with two grooves, one for each child's writing tool; seat and back of seat made from slats; iron bolts hold the piece together; again, as in most early school desks, the seat is for the child (or as here, the children) using the desk in front — the desk services the child sitting on next seat behind this one; (looks like a mud dauber has discovered this piece as it shows a great deal of outside exposure); there is a short iron groove-centered rail at each side down far enough from the desk top where a shelf for books (now missing) was provided.

Schoolmaster's Desk
ca. 1810-1840
H.30", at top, W.21".
"Fall-Front," "Drop Front," or "Slant-Front" writing
surface. Knob drawer pulls; two wide boards on top
with narrow third for a shelf; found in Virginia.

School Desk
ca. 1800's
H.31", W.2⅜", Depth 16½".
Slant-lid top; glass inkwell with cover; molding
around edges and a one-board stretcher (for books
or footrest).

Store "Till" Box Desk
ca. 1800's
H.5" up to 7½", W.21¾", Depth 17".
Molded edges of two-board lid; whittled out keyhole, no key; large inside
storage space; lid is writing surface.

Table Desk
ca. 1800's
Carefully handmade on the northeast coast of Florida;
pivot-latch holding closed a side dropdoor inside
cubicle; large writing surface; the typical straight legs
of pine "country" pieces.

Lap (Travel) Desk
ca. 1850
H.8½", W.21½", Depth 10".
Lacquered black over walnut, the primary wood; this enameling was the American answer to Far Eastern finishes. (Shown here to illustrate: even after pine was acknowledged and became widely used as a primary wood, it was still in demand for such as interior divisions where it easily accommodated more difficult fittings than would have been possible from harder woods, the pine readily lending itself to faster and better cuttings.) This original walnut box has stenciled designs; inside blind dovetailed corners and green felt writing surface on the drop piece with the leather flap; it is 20½" wide when opened flat to write; four small and one large (papers) area.

Dry Sinks

Dry Sink
ca. 1800's
H.33", W.43" at top, 42" at base, ½" molding around top edge, sink well recessed 4", 20" wide.
Shaped feet and apron center; paneled doors conceal two storage shelves; porcelain knobs replacements; the no-ticeable imperfections (no minus at all in value) first attributed to rodent entry-attempts are actually the settings of the original latches. (For interest, the sink is now kept in the dining room of a restored early home; atop are an iron fishtail scale with brass arm and basket, computing 25 lbs., with the label "Made by Burrow, Stuart, Milne, Hamilton, Ontario"; also a brass store lamp (newly electrified) with its original milkglass shade and clear chimney, both found at Wilson, NY.)

Dry Sink
ca. 1880
H.33½", W.42¼", Depth 24".
German pine; lift top amazingly still has the original gray enamel washpans
(dishpans) with a deep open well below reaching to the bottom shelf of the
sink; brass keykeepers; iron hinges to raise the overhang top; has a
decorative dentil (dentelle) (serrated) molding on the front panel.

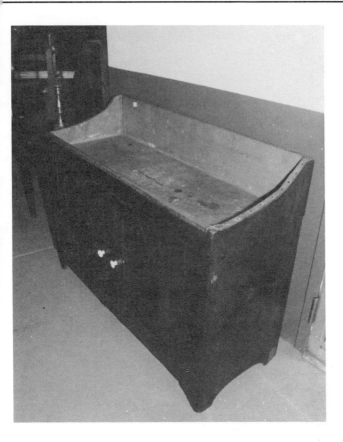

Dry Sink
ca. 1830-1840
H.39", W.50", Depth 18", recessed sink 2¾".
All original handfashioned in Pennsylvania; original brick red paint now darkened; porcelain knobs, two shelves inside wide doors; sloping sides back to splashboard. Rare to find one with the original zinc, this truly properly called a "Zinc Bench" and in fine condition.

Dry Sink (Zinc Bench)
ca. 1840
H.36¾", W.53½", Depth 21½".
Ohio handmade; original red color dimmed but still pretty; this from a skilled worker (large workshops turned out a great many from the first quarter of the 1800's until the 1880's, reproductions still being made); Smithy-made iron hinges; molding trim and beveled doors concealing storage shelves; doors whose pull knobs (Shakers called them "pegs") have extended straight lengths through the doors, held inside by round whittled pins; a zinc-lined well held dishpans when there were no water inlets nor drains in homes; a slanted four-side gallery about 8½" high at back and 5½" at front were splashboards protecting walls — and preventing dishwashers' aprons from becoming too liberally doused. Folks often still said "work at the zinc" (sink) even long after actual water-supplied indoor "sinks" became commonplace.

Dry Sink
ca. 1850
H.32" at front, 36" at back, W.42½", Depth 18½". Well is about 29" wide, 16" deep and 5" recessed.
From a home at Hansen, Idaho. Original pine knobs are replaced with porcelain; small pull drawer at side of
wall and storage shelves behind closed doors below; feet shaped from sides and front framing boards.

Racks

Pie Cooling Rack
ca. 1800's
Shaker-style from Pennsylvania. H.69", space from front uprights to that at rear is 22½".
Entirely held together with wooden pins, those at the back, 4" long, support the pie coolers inserted on the shelves as well as hold the two supports extending from the bottom crossbar 11" up from the floor and the other 9" from the top to the back upright, firming the handcrafted structure; 18 dowel-type rounds making the cooling shelves are slashed into the side uprights; it's an interesting and unusual piece that is best used when placed in a corner.

Pie Cooling Boards
ca. 1800's
These are from Pennsylvania but they originated in France. Handmade wooden discs have individual differences;
all, however, have handles (with hanging holes) cut as one-piece with the coolers; two wooden bands inserted into
each were to help prevent warping, although there has already been some age shrinkage, as seen in the ends of the
inserted boards slightly protruding beyond the cooler proper. Sizes shown:
L.26", 21½" across at center, 1" wide inserted bands.
L.24¼", 19½" across at center, 1" wide inserted bands.
L.25½", 21¼" across at center, ⅝" wide inserted bands.
L.24", 19½" across at center, 1¼" wide insertedbands.

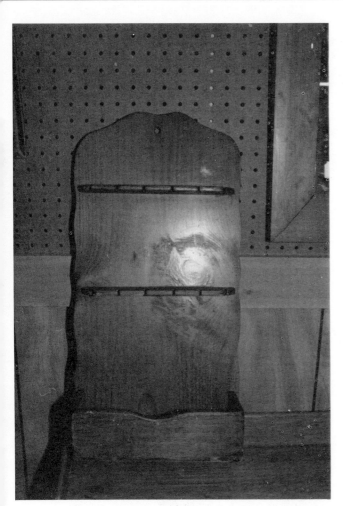

Spoon Rack
ca. early 1800's
H.22", W.14".
Ten spaces; open well at the bottom with carved top could have held cleaning materials for the spoons. No doubt many were made of pewter.

Spoon and Knife Rack
ca. 1700's
H.20½", W.30¾", Depth 6½".
Wall hung; spoon slots in front, knife slots at the sides; hand-crafted; small pullout drawer at middle front, porcelain knob has been replaced; handfashioned with considerable skill; well at top center holds a stoneware mortar and pestle as originally intended; Tennessee origin.

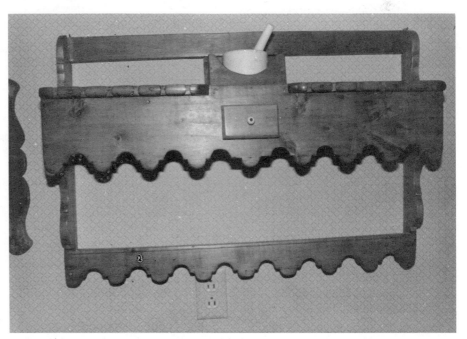

Quilt/Blanket Racks
ca. 1800-1820
No stained or whitened areas that indicate usage as drying racks, but it's possible they were used as such. Seen at Ransomville, NY; original green paint; extremely heavy base (they look upside down but aren't); each rounded topside upright is penetrated with one end of the two turned crosspieces that held the bedding.

Stands and Tables

Field (Campaign) Table
ca. 1700's
H.15", W.35½", Depth 18".
During the American Revolutionary War, this table belonging to Officer Jeremiah Townsend was kept in his field tent in New York State's Hudson River Valley. Carried from home, or handmade by their Headquarter's Troops Blacksmith, the splayed four legs (one a bit more angled out than the other three) are slashed through the top and pins inserted for extra rigidity. Sharp table corners have been angle-cut and the edges smoothed for making fewer bump-bruises in tent space notoriously limited.

Folk Art Table/Desk
ca. 1870's
H.30½", W.50½", Depth 26¼".
Unusual styling (conforming to a given style rather than to a natural state). Seen in Lake Ontario region at Clarence, New York; the pear-shaped ornamentations at the rear edge could also have been put there practically to keep things from sliding off backwards; the "pears" sit on short dowel pins and can simply be lifted off; each "pear" is 4¾" high, 4⅛" in diameter at the widest part; flat button turned legs.

Dining Table
ca. 1800's
H.29½", L.76¾".
A four-sides 6" apron; four-board table top. Polished to a handsome glow; small drawer near the table end on one side has a replaced porcelain knob; Penn./NY State origin.

Close-up of dining table leg.

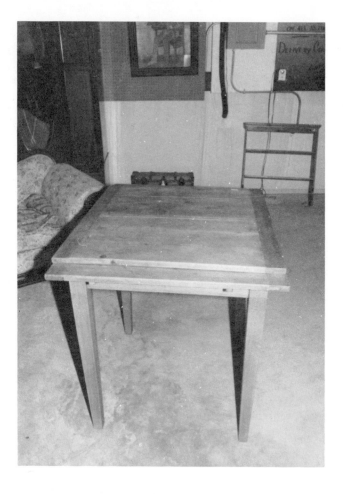

Table (Dinette, Extension)
ca. early 1900's
H.32", L.31½", W.30".
Breadboard sides; 13" wood pin held board at each
end that could be pulled out and then up flush with the
table top; with the advent of these smaller dining tables
just after the turn of the century the phrase "dinette"
became popular along with the piece, convenient in
smaller homes.

Table
An old one.
H.24⅞", W.25½", Depth 13½".
Primitive "woodshed project"; still ably supports wide overhanging top
though one stretcher end could use a nail; random width four-board top;
a nice little table holding onto its original blue point.

Kitchen Table
ca. 1800's
H.29½". W.36",
Depth 23".
Georgia heartpine; breadboard tabletop ends; about a 4" apron on four sides; tapered legs (straight legs most typical of early pine pieces). No matter the age, breadboard construction indicates better quality — the grain of the end boards, as here, always running in the opposite direction from that of the parent pieces in the furniture — to prevent warping.

Table (Kitchen)
ca. 1840-1850
H.29, W.34", L.48½".
Mississippi heartpine; two-board top, one drawer; pegged construction; tapered legs.

Table
H.29½", L.35", W.29".
Louisiana southern hardpine; long end of table drawer dovetailed four corners and has self knob; light natural color.

Midwestern Table
H.28½", W.34",
Depth 18¼".
One narrow drawer with walnut stained knob; fine quality early 2-board top.

Side Table
ca. 1800
L.72", Depth 25".
English pine; kitchen table type; time and usage worn; two gnawings at the back of three self-knob drawers which are irregularly dovetailed at their four corners; one low stretcher each side between front and back legs; extra wide aprons; overhang top.

Back view of side table.

Tavern Table
ca. 1800's
H.26", Dia.22½".
Southern pine; grooved top edges; small apron; pegged squared straight legs with four connecting stretchers which would have made good footrests.

Table
ca. 1890's-1900
H.29", W.22", Depth 22⅞".
Two-board top hanging down one side, a result of warping — both overhanging the apron sides; dark stained; dealer offered reasonably "as is."

Auctioneer's Pedestal
ca. 1800's
Two sections; top H.26".
20" x 20" square cabinet under a heavily molded cornice with a similarly built base is groove-paneled on each side; a two-hinged front door opens with its dark metal pull knob into a deep hollow storage compartment which can also be reached by lifting the narrow top half of the cornice; pullout shelves at middle each have two small brass knobs; the lower section — a sides-paneled portion H.26", W.25", Depth 27" has a 10" high dovetailed corners platform for standing. Thoughtful and attractive features have been incorporated in this handcrafted piece of pine furniture.

Stand/Table
H.28½", W.21½", Depth 15¼".
From an early Erie County, NY estate; handfashioned pine with a cherry front on one of the four corners dovetailed drawers; large wooden knobs.

Cutting Table (Butcher's Block/ Meat Block)
H.30", W.29½", Depth 18".
Amish from Adamstown, Penn.; an old one; a particularly good size, fits well into modern rooms; southern hard pine with a laminated top.

Crock Cooling Stand
(Today used extensively used for displays)
ca. 1800's (a Pennsylvania piece)
Bottom shelf straight across measures W.46", third shelf is W.35", second shelf is W.21", and the top shelf is W.16".
Held by three one-board braces cut as stairsteps to accommodate the shelves; when crocks (pottery or stoneware) came out of a kiln, they were placed on some type of stand for cooling.

Washstand
ca. 1800's
H.29½", Square top 17".
Combined wood legs; three-side gallery on shelf below.

Umbrella/Parasol Stand
ca. 1800's
H.27", 15¼" widest part.
Pine with oak combination; tin drip plate in base for wet umbrellas.

Washstand
ca. 1870
Stripped and wax finished; two doors with molded trims that were originally key-opened; two self-knob drawers; ball-turned feet; elaborate stiles (front side uprights) have a Victorian feeling. Between ca. 1855 and 1880, this Victorian style was called the "Renaissance Revival" or "Grand Rapids Revival" with so many manufacturers there using the vastly important and popular marble surfaces of the period.

Trunks

Trunks from years past performed the same as those today, containers of indeterminate styles and sizes — boxes or chests holding clothing, bedding or whatever the need — kept in homes for permanent storage or as carriers for moving goods.

Immigrant's Trunk
ca. 1800's
H.12½", W.21½", Depth 12".
Handforged hardware and iron firming straps; white brush script (similar to calligraphy); Scandinavian origin with destination "Minneola Lyon Minnesota," second line obliterated except for "America."

Blanket Chest/Trunk
ca. 1700's
H.35", W.39", Depth 26".
Dovetailed four corners; iron straps liberally reinforce the chest (suggesting it was moved about frequently, even held bedding and more on a settler's migration farther west); much ornamentation in the shaping of the iron strap hinges across the bowed heavy lid, round buttons holding fast all the strapping; graceful center three-pronged decoration continues down to meet the animal-like head stamped on the over-large plate key keeper (equalized in size to the overall trunk dimensions) having an iron lift ring and keyhole for locking below that. An excellent example of quality handcrafting; care in treatment through the years from the owners; and it's of Pennsylvania origin.

Dome Top Child's Trunk
ca. 1840
H.14⅞" at center lid, W.26", Depth 13½".
Snap-down iron catch could originally be locked; iron strapping; three iron rosette-held wood strips decorate lid top; inside had originally been paper lined along with tray inside, but both have had stains from dampness.

Circus Trunk
ca. 1800's
H.21½", W.54¼", Depth 23½".
The way it is decorated reminds one of a circus, don't you think? Makes for memories — sawdust rings, street parades ending with the fabulous shrill calliopes! Handfashioned with chamfered top.

Captain's Sea Chest
ca. 1850's
H.20½", W.30½", Depth 22½".
Handforged iron fixtures; inside are varied size drawers with one long one as a "till" for valuables, all having a flat wood cover to prevent contents from rolling out in heavy seas; drawers have tiny brass knobs; four dovetailed corners reinforced with iron straps.

On Top of Chest
6½" Dia. wrapped and lidded box, original green paint on pine.

Checkerboard
ca. late 1800's (Victorian)
Board is slate, found at Wiscasset, Maine; surface was scratched, and then the lines filled in with India Ink — reds, black and browns.

Wooden Checkers
ca. 1910
Origin Prince Edward Island, Canada.
Wood worn smooth from handling.

Dower Chest
ca. early 1800's
H.28½", W.47¼", Depth 26½", base H.23".
Pennsylvania Dutch (German) origin.
Still has faint blue original paint; molded edge bow (dome) three-board top; overall woodpegged construction; Smithy-forged iron handles each side; strap side reinforcements and a trace of an old iron latch decor on top; remains of circle trims at front.

Painted Chest
ca. 1879 (seen at front)
H.39", W.18¾", Depth 18¾".
Painted red and black with white — rope and flower designs; lightly curved
top with three sides overhanging; name "H.M. Olsen"; inside is a lidded box
W.5½", H.4" on a side shelf; believed to be Norwegian.

Immigrant's Trunk
ca. 1734 A.D.
"C.J. Peterson's" appears in dim black paint inside one drawer. Found at Kansas estate sale; rear view only due to inaccessibility during a show's setup; several inside side drawers; outside near one edge is a 1" wide strip of original red paint seen through overall false graining, both finishes of which, happily, are still obvious under a coat of colorless sealer the present owner added for preservation; base slants upward to a border overhang domed top; its keykeeper, as all the hardware, is handforged in the shape of a three-top curved heart; dovetailed four corners with tiny shaped strap iron to hold; back iron straps extend full height as they do at front, the back extending into hinges; side iron handgrips.

Immigrant's Trunk
ca. 1850's
H.18", W.31½", Depth 17½".
Dome top; original green paint on pine; black German script giving name and destination no longer readable — just enough you know it was there; iron side carrying handles; key and keeper gone.

"Jenny Lind" Trunk
ca. 1850
H.15½", W.28", Widest depth at base 17½".
Domed top; New Hampshire origin. All original; notable shape; solid brass banding with black iron mid-band; brass buttons ornamental as well as necessary; stitched leather round handgrip to raise lid, anchored each end with two brass buttons; handsome brass lion's head stamp-embossed on swinging keyhole cover, the lion and keyhole on a distinctive brass plate; side leather lift handles.

Close-up of swinging keyhole cover on the Jenny Lind Trunk.

Small Trunk
ca. 1840's
H.16½" W.24½," Depth 14".
Dovetailed each corner with added short iron bands and new latch added sometime later; note signs of original whittled out keyhole; Southern pine; a primitive.

Close-up of whittled out keyhole in the small trunk.

Travel Trunk
ca. 1800's
Strap iron banded; brass buttons; original lock, no key.

Flat Top Trunk
ca. 1840's
H.13", W.25", Depth 15".
Has been stripped but color shows it had been previously painted white; dovetailed four corners; iron side handles.

Complementing the Furniture

Berry Bucket (Shaker Made)
ca. 1800's
Staved pine, iron bail (handle) and handcut handgrip. Age-faded green over rarer original so-called "Shaker Blue," also known as "Amish Blue," a small part of indigo dye added according to worker's custom of mixing to a larger amount of white. Shaker blues varied, from the pale grayish shade as here to much brighter sky blues.

Bowl
ca. 1840
Uncommonly large; Dia. 26", Depth 9".
Fashioned from one piece of pine; 1½" thick band carved
around the rim; handsome graining. New England origin.

Dough Bowl
ca. 1880
L.54¼", W.18", Depth 8".
German pine; handles vary from 2½" to 3" in length. Probably a baker's bowl.

Butter Churn
ca. 1800's
H.31", L.25", Depth 19".
Owner's refinishing to natural pine color still left stubborn flecks of original green paint; the domed lid fits inside a top churn groove; self knob lift; four-section inside paddle can be taken out for removing butter and cleaning, held by an iron outside turn-bar with a wood handgrip; today the churn handsomely decorates a home's foyer.

Butter Churn (Dasher Type)
ca. 1800's
Top dia. of churn 6¾", base 9"; with handle H.37½",
churn H.16"; handle worn where gripped for churning
butter.
Three metal bands; found in Ohio; traces of old base
blue paint; has a heavy and more uncommon type of lift
off splash collar; stamped on underside (made by)
"G.M.A. Wilder, So. Bingham, Mass."; round holes in
crisscross pieces at bottom of handle to form the dasher.

Butter Churn
ca. later 1800's
Top dia. of church about 7", with handle H.36½".
Two wrapped wood bands at top; three heavy wire
bands below. Dasher has the bottom flat crisscross
wood agitators with holes to allow freer movement of
cream through the blades while cream is being
churned. (One owner called this furniture a good
"place" for odds and ends.)

Butter Churn (Handle Turn Type)
ca. 1900 (resembles a style patented ca. 1870's).
H.28½", top 14"x14½".
This seems to be an old churn put on new legs. Pine
with a rolled metal bottom; the original drainage holes
have been plugged; lacks the iron handle and inside
paddles. (Owner enjoys as a kitchen piece which is a
good "stash-away" place.)

Food Grater
ca. 1800-1810
L.14", W.9", Depth 3½".
Handfashioned rarity found in a barn at Cape Cod.
One-board back, ¾" thick wood construction; self
pull knob opens full length drawer for emptying the
grated foods which have fallen through the punched
tin; a soft age-patina (satiny, mellowed surface appearance wood acquires with age and usage); two-
corners' firming rawhide repairs that were later
added when needed; hole carved in handle-hold-
shaped end indicates the grater could be wall hung
when not in use.

Cranberry Picker
ca. 1800's
Length almost 9" when closed, W.8½", handle attached one end at center 3¼" deep; from its size, thought to have been for women workers. New England origin with owner's initial "T" cut into pine side; opened and closed on two bent brass straps, held closed by a small brass clip, clamping down the cover, holding harvest berries inside on a base felt-cushioned to retard bruising; 22 long iron teeth 6¾"L. gathered in the red goodies (puckery-sour until sugared) from the bushes.

Plantation Shutters
ca. 1830
H.49", W.17" each.
Handmade from random width boards, wood pegged; one front and one reverse side shown; initials cut in are "W.F."; smithy forged iron strap hinges on pivots (Gudgeons); wood pinned (or pegged) cross pieces holding intact the upright boards.

Sifter
ca. 1800's
H.28½", W.16¼", Depth 3½".
Pennsylvania piece; Bakers' flour and/or sugar sifter; its pine frame has hand-shaped holds for carrying and better handling; an unusual prettily-punched tin center. This indeed is a quality pine artifact.

Sifter
L.9⅛", H.6".
From earlier 1800's in Ohio.
Metal banded rolled-edge liftoff top; the ultra-fine wire screen covers the bottom under the handturned flat wood sifter paddles; released flour drifts into a container set at the base of this kitchen helper; and again, pine is used since it transmitted no taste nor odor to the susceptible flour.

Winnowing Tray
ca. 1800's
L.51", Width 23", sides 9½" deep.
White pine; generous bentwood carrying handles; four-board base; also called a "Winnowing Basket"; used here as wall decoration; others have had legs added to use them as a table, not a drastic change to the original form.

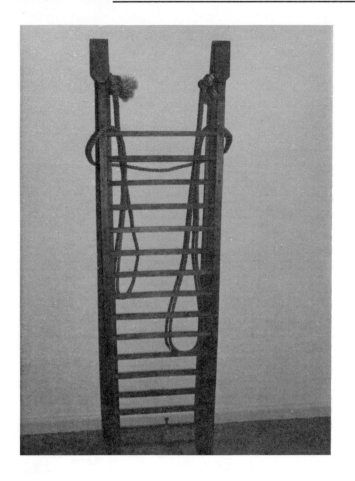

Work Pull Sled
ca. 1800's
L.56", 1¾" wide iron strap runners. Side woods are each ⅞" thick, 4½" wide.
New England origin. Still has the original hemp rope fastened through holes on each front side; 17 squared crosspieces (squared to better hold wood pieces) tapered-whittled at either end to penetrate the wood sides.

Work Pull Sled shown with a practical modern usage.

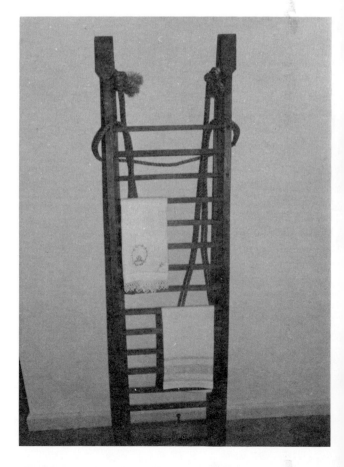

Accessories in Pine

Mirror
ca. 1840
H.33", W.17½".
White pine frame; original glass; two-board raw wood back also of pine.

Door
ca. late 1800's
H.83", W.36".
Pine and oak; will have to have a knob; front panel has mark where original doorbell was attached.

Rocking Seat
ca. 1900
For a baby as soon as it could sit and as long as it could fit into the carpet-tapestry-design cloth-padded space between two white horses; colorfully eye-catching harness and saddle, all still in the original paints; wood base and rockers.

Hobbyhorse
ca. 1920
L.33½", seat W.4½".
Red painted with black trim Rocking Horse; operates forward and back on dowels, springs, and wood base.

Poster Rack
ca. after 1900
H.47", W.28¼".
Surprisingly sturdy; bottom brace set out far enough to accommodate the approximate thickness of poster board and so the owner names it. In a humble home, it might have served as a corner stand for a treasured family picture not able to be expensively framed.

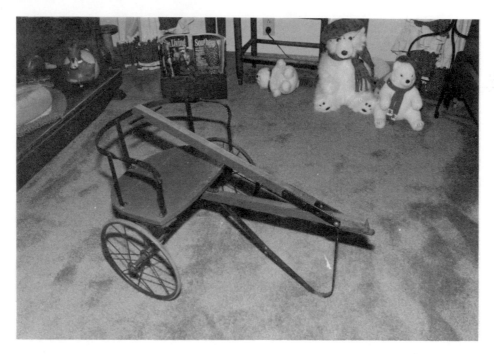

Pull Cart
ca. 1920's
Overall H.33", W.14", Depth 10¾"; seat is H.10".
Pine wood and black painted iron with wire wheels having wire spokes and rubber tires; repainted to the original barn-red some time ago.

Child's Sled/Sleigh
ca. 1800's
L.35¼" from black painted
wooden handle bar to the top of
the curved footrest (decorative
current style); simulating adults'
sleighs; widest part 14½", a comfortable size for a small child
even with its bulky "bundling
up."

These were easily pushed across
the ice (ponds, etc.) while parents also enjoyed themselves on
ice-skates, sort of a last century
Victorian family togetherness.
Original white paint still clings
with black outline trims and now
almost invisible flower clusters,
once bright, on each side; iron
bands firm the handle to the
back of the sled and wooden
runners have attached iron on
the bottoms.

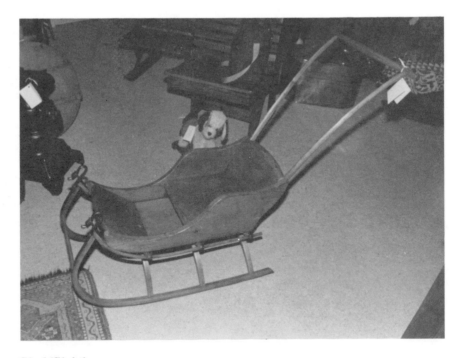

Sled/Sleigh
ca. 1860
Height with handle 33", W.11", seat length 51" overall.
Could be pushed or pulled behind as the nurse or parents ice-skated
along; turned up footrest with fanciful curved neck swan heads complet-
ing the iron runners attached to the bottom of the wooden ones.

Sled
ca. 1800's
H.6", L.28", W.10½".
Pennsylvania origin near Lancaster; original red paint almost obliterated; held together with ¾" diameter dowel pins; two iron underside crosspieces holding sides and supporting the seat; two iron straps further braced each side when the sled began to crack; originally had iron runners set into grooves beneath; hand-length slots provided easier carrying; hemp ropes tied at front were the "pulls."

Pull Sled
ca. 1900
H.3", L.33½", W.12½".
Tennessee origin; still has considerable amount of weathered original white paint left; four slats; heavy iron wire inset into wood are the runners — curved at front — holding hammered-in wire loops to attach the pull rope; sides handholds for easier carrying.

Stepladder
ca. 1900
Every home — or almost every — at the turn of the century had one of these Old Faithfuls, made from thick hard pine with iron fixtures at both sides permitting opening and closing flat. Seen as a For Sale display at an antiques show, it was also on duty at home between shows, there being so many ways to decoratively use these today.

Viola Case
ca. 1700's-early 1800's
H.51", Width at base 19¼", Depth 8¾".
From a long-time American collection; originally found in the hills of Scotland; entirely handmade; handforged hardware.

Interior of Viola Case shown.

Index and Values